AF096696

Website:
Username:
Password:
Notes:

* * * *

Website:
Username:
Password:
Notes:

* * * *

Website:
Username:
Password:
Notes:

A

Website: _____

Username: _____

Password: _____

Notes: _____

_____

_____

_____

✳ ✳ ✳ ✳

Website: _____

Username: _____

Password: _____

Notes: _____

_____

_____

_____

✳ ✳ ✳ ✳

Website: _____

Username: _____

Password: _____

Notes: _____

_____

_____

_____

Website:

Username:

Password:

Notes:

✳ ✳ ✳ ✳

Website:

Username:

Password:

Notes:

✳ ✳ ✳ ✳

Website:

Username:

Password:

Notes:

YZ

Website:

Username:

Password:

Notes:

* * * *

Website:

Username:

Password:

Notes:

* * * *

Website:

Username:

Password:

Notes:

Website:
Username:
Password:
Notes:

* * * *

Website:
Username:
Password:
Notes:

* * * *

Website:
Username:
Password:
Notes:

YZ

Website:

Username:

Password:

Notes:

* * * *

Website:

Username:

Password:

Notes:

* * * *

Website:

Username:

Password:

Notes:

Website:

Username:

Password:

Notes:

* * * *

Website:

Username:

Password:

Notes:

* * * *

Website:

Username:

Password:

Notes:

Website:

Username:

Password:

Notes:

✷ ✷ ✷ ✷

Website:

Username:

Password:

Notes:

✷ ✷ ✷ ✷

Website:

Username:

Password:

Notes:

WX

Website:

Username:

Password:

Notes:

* * * *

Website:

Username:

Password:

Notes:

* * * *

Website:

Username:

Password:

Notes:

Website: _____

Username: _____

Password: _____

Notes: _____

_____

_____

_____

※ ※ ※ ※

Website: _____

Username: _____

Password: _____

Notes: _____

_____

_____

_____

※ ※ ※ ※

Website: _____

Username: _____

Password: _____

Notes: _____

_____

_____

_____

Website:

Username:

Password:

Notes:

* * * *

Website:

Username:

Password:

Notes:

* * * *

Website:

Username:

Password:

Notes:

Website:
Username:
Password:
Notes:

* * * *

Website:
Username:
Password:
Notes:

* * * *

Website:
Username:
Password:
Notes:

uv

Website:

Username:

Password:

Notes:

* * * *

Website:

Username:

Password:

Notes:

* * * *

Website:

Username:

Password:

Notes:

UV

Website:

Username:

Password:

Notes:

* * * *

Website:

Username:

Password:

Notes:

* * * *

Website:

Username:

Password:

Notes:

uv

Website:

Username:

Password:

Notes:

* * * *

Website:

Username:

Password:

Notes:

* * * *

Website:

Username:

Password:

Notes:

Website: _____

Username: _____

Password: _____

Notes: _____

_____

_____

_____

✷ ✷ ✷ ✷

Website: _____

Username: _____

Password: _____

Notes: _____

_____

_____

_____

✷ ✷ ✷ ✷

Website: _____

Username: _____

Password: _____

Notes: _____

_____

_____

_____

T

Website:

Username:

Password:

Notes:

* * * *

Website:

Username:

Password:

Notes:

* * * *

Website:

Username:

Password:

Notes:

Website:
Username:
Password:
Notes:

* * * *

Website:
Username:
Password:
Notes:

* * * *

Website:
Username:
Password:
Notes:

Website:

Username:

Password:

Notes:

* * * *

Website:

Username:

Password:

Notes:

* * * *

Website:

Username:

Password:

Notes:

Website:

Username:

Password:

Notes:

✳ ✳ ✳ ✳

Website:

Username:

Password:

Notes:

✳ ✳ ✳ ✳

Website:

Username:

Password:

Notes:

Website:

Username:

Password:

Notes:

✳ ✳ ✳ ✳

Website:

Username:

Password:

Notes:

✳ ✳ ✳ ✳

Website:

Username:

Password:

Notes:

Website:

Username:

Password:

Notes:

* * * *

Website:

Username:

Password:

Notes:

* * * *

Website:

Username:

Password:

Notes:

Website:
Username:
Password:
Notes:

* * * *

Website:
Username:
Password:
Notes:

* * * *

QR

Website:
Username:
Password:
Notes:

Website:

Username:

Password:

Notes:

* * * *

Website:

Username:

Password:

Notes:

* * * *

Website:

Username:

Password:

Notes:

QR

Website:

Username:

Password:

Notes:

✳ ✳ ✳ ✳

Website:

Username:

Password:

Notes:

✳ ✳ ✳ ✳

Website:

Username:

Password:

Notes:

Website: _____
Username: _____
Password: _____
Notes: _____
_____
_____
_____

✳ ✳ ✳ ✳

Website: _____
Username: _____
Password: _____
Notes: _____
_____
_____
_____

✳ ✳ ✳ ✳

Website: _____
Username: _____
Password: _____
Notes: _____
_____
_____
_____

QR

Website:

Username:

Password:

Notes:

* * * *

Website:

Username:

Password:

Notes:

* * * *

Website:

Username:

Password:

Notes:

Website:

Username:

Password:

Notes:

* * * *

Website:

Username:

Password:

Notes:

* * * *

Website:

Username:

Password:

Notes:

Website:
Username:
Password:
Notes:

* * * *

Website:
Username:
Password:
Notes:

* * * *

Website:
Username:
Password:
Notes:

Website:

Username:

Password:

Notes:

* * * *

Website:

Username:

Password:

Notes:

* * * *

Website:

Username:

Password:

Notes:

Website:

Username:

Password:

Notes:

* * * *

Website:

Username:

Password:

Notes:

* * * *

Website:

Username:

Password:

Notes:

Website:

Username:

Password:

Notes:

* * * *

Website:

Username:

Password:

Notes:

* * * *

Website:

Username:

Password:

Notes:

Website:

Username:

Password:

Notes:

* * * *

Website:

Username:

Password:

Notes:

* * * *

Website:

Username:

Password:

Notes:

Website: _____
Username: _____
Password: _____
Notes: _____
_____
_____
_____

✳ ✳ ✳ ✳

Website: _____
Username: _____
Password: _____
Notes: _____
_____
_____
_____

✳ ✳ ✳ ✳

Website: _____
Username: _____
Password: _____
Notes: _____
_____
_____
_____

Website:

Username:

Password:

Notes:

* * * *

Website:

Username:

Password:

Notes:

* * * *

Website:

Username:

Password:

Notes:

Website:

Username:

Password:

Notes:

* * * *

Website:

Username:

Password:

Notes:

* * * *

Website:

Username:

Password:

Notes:

Website:

Username:

Password:

Notes:

* * * *

Website:

Username:

Password:

Notes:

* * * *

Website:

Username:

Password:

Notes:

Website:

Username:

Password:

Notes:

* * * *

Website:

Username:

Password:

Notes:

* * * *

Website:

Username:

Password:

Notes:

Website:

Username:

Password:

Notes:

* * * *

Website:

Username:

Password:

Notes:

* * * *

Website:

Username:

Password:

Notes:

Website:

Username:

Password:

Notes:

* * * *

Website:

Username:

Password:

Notes:

M

* * * *

Website:

Username:

Password:

Notes:

Website:

Username:

Password:

Notes:

* * * *

Website:

Username:

Password:

Notes:

M

* * * *

Website:

Username:

Password:

Notes:

Website:

Username:

Password:

Notes:

* * * *

Website:

Username:

Password:

Notes:

M

* * * *

Website:

Username:

Password:

Notes:

Website:

Username:

Password:

Notes:

* * * *

Website:

Username:

Password:

Notes:

* * * *

Website:

Username:

Password:

Notes:

Website: _____

Username: _____

Password: _____

Notes: _____

_____

_____

_____

✳ ✳ ✳ ✳

Website: _____

Username: _____

Password: _____

Notes: _____

_____

_____

_____

L

✳ ✳ ✳ ✳

Website: _____

Username: _____

Password: _____

Notes: _____

_____

_____

_____

Website:

Username:

Password:

Notes:

* * * *

Website:

Username:

Password:

Notes:

* * * *

Website:

Username:

Password:

Notes:

Website:

Username:

Password:

Notes:

✳ ✳ ✳ ✳

Website:

Username:

Password:

Notes:

L

✳ ✳ ✳ ✳

Website:

Username:

Password:

Notes:

Website:
Username:
Password:
Notes:

* * * *

Website:
Username:
Password:
Notes:

* * * *

Website:
Username:
Password:
Notes:

Website:

Username:

Password:

Notes:

* * * *

Website:

Username:

Password:

Notes:

* * * *

Website:

Username:

Password:

Notes:

Website:

Username:

Password:

Notes:

✴ ✴ ✴ ✴

Website:

Username:

Password:

Notes:

✴ ✴ ✴ ✴

Website:

Username:

Password:

Notes:

Website:

Username:

Password:

Notes:

* * * *

Website:

Username:

Password:

Notes:

* * * *

Website:

Username:

Password:

Notes:

Website:

Username:

Password:

Notes:

* * * *

IJ

Website:

Username:

Password:

Notes:

* * * *

Website:

Username:

Password:

Notes:

Website:

Username:

Password:

Notes:

* * * *

IJ

Website:

Username:

Password:

Notes:

* * * *

Website:

Username:

Password:

Notes:

IJ

Website:

Username:

Password:

Notes:

* * * *

Website:

Username:

Password:

Notes:

* * * *

Website:

Username:

Password:

Notes:

Website:

Username:

Password:

Notes:

* * * *

IJ

Website:

Username:

Password:

Notes:

* * * *

Website:

Username:

Password:

Notes:

Website:

Username:

Password:

Notes:

✶ ✶ ✶ ✶

Website:

Username:

Password:

Notes:

✶ ✶ ✶ ✶

Website:

Username:

Password:

Notes:

Website:

Username:

Password:

Notes:

* * * *

Website:

Username:

Password:

Notes:

* * * *

Website:

Username:

Password:

Notes:

Website:

Username:

Password:

Notes:

* * * *

Website:

Username:

Password:

Notes:

* * * *

Website:

Username:

Password:

Notes:

Website:

Username:

Password:

Notes:

* * * *

Website:

Username:

Password:

Notes:

* * * *

Website:

Username:

Password:

Notes:

Website:
Username:
Password:
Notes:

G

* * * *

Website:
Username:
Password:
Notes:

* * * *

Website:
Username:
Password:
Notes:

Website:
Username:
Password:
Notes:

G

* * * *

Website:
Username:
Password:
Notes:

* * * *

Website:
Username:
Password:
Notes:

Website:

Username:

Password:

Notes:

* * * *

Website:

Username:

Password:

Notes:

* * * *

Website:

Username:

Password:

Notes:

Website: www.gooseberrypatch.com

Username:

Password:

Notes: gooseberrypatch.typepad.com

facebook.com/gooseberrypatch

twitter.com/gooseberrypatch

youtube.com/gooseberrypatchcom

G

✳ ✳ ✳ ✳

Website:

Username:

Password:

Notes:

✳ ✳ ✳ ✳

Website:

Username:

Password:

Notes:

Website:

Username:

Password:

Notes:

* * * *

Website:

Username:

Password:

Notes:

* * * *

Website:

Username:

Password:

Notes:

Website:

Username:

Password:

Notes:

EF

✶ ✶ ✶ ✶

Website:

Username:

Password:

Notes:

✶ ✶ ✶ ✶

Website:

Username:

Password:

Notes:

Website:

Username:

Password:

Notes:

* * * *

Website:

Username:

Password:

Notes:

* * * *

Website:

Username:

Password:

Notes:

Website:

Username:

Password:

Notes:

EF

* * * *

Website:

Username:

Password:

Notes:

* * * *

Website:

Username:

Password:

Notes:

Website:
Username:
Password:
Notes:

* * * *

Website:
Username:
Password:
Notes:

* * * *

Website:
Username:
Password:
Notes:

Website:

Username:

Password:

Notes:

D

* * * *

Website:

Username:

Password:

Notes:

* * * *

Website:

Username:

Password:

Notes:

D

Website:
Username:
Password:
Notes:

* * * *

Website:
Username:
Password:
Notes:

* * * *

Website:
Username:
Password:
Notes:

D

Website:
Username:
Password:
Notes:

* * * *

Website:
Username:
Password:
Notes:

* * * *

Website:
Username:
Password:
Notes:

Website:

Username:

Password:

Notes:

✳ ✳ ✳ ✳

Website:

Username:

Password:

Notes:

✳ ✳ ✳ ✳

Website:

Username:

Password:

Notes:

Website: _____

Username: _____

Password: _____

Notes: _____

_____

_____

_____

C

✻ ✻ ✻ ✻

Website: _____

Username: _____

Password: _____

Notes: _____

_____

_____

_____

✻ ✻ ✻ ✻

Website: _____

Username: _____

Password: _____

Notes: _____

_____

_____

_____

C

Website:

Username:

Password:

Notes:

* * * *

Website:

Username:

Password:

Notes:

* * * *

Website:

Username:

Password:

Notes:

Website:

Username:

Password:

Notes:

* * * *

Website:

Username:

Password:

Notes:

* * * *

Website:

Username:

Password:

Notes:

B

Website:

Username:

Password:

Notes:

* * * *

Website:

Username:

Password:

Notes:

* * * *

Website:

Username:

Password:

Notes:

Website: _____
Username: _____
Password: _____
Notes: _____
_____
_____
_____

✳ ✳ ✳ ✳

Website: _____
Username: _____
Password: _____
Notes: _____
_____
_____
_____

✳ ✳ ✳ ✳

Website: _____
Username: _____
Password: _____
Notes: _____
_____
_____
_____

B

Website:

Username:

Password:

Notes:

✳ ✳ ✳ ✳

Website:

Username:

Password:

Notes:

✳ ✳ ✳ ✳

Website:

Username:

Password:

Notes:

Website:

Username:

Password:

Notes:

* * * *

Website:

Username:

Password:

Notes:

* * * *

Website:

Username:

Password:

Notes:

Website:
Username:
Password:
Notes:

✱ ✱ ✱ ✱

Website:
Username:
Password:
Notes:

✱ ✱ ✱ ✱

Website:
Username:
Password:
Notes:

A

Website: _____

Username: _____

Password: _____

Notes: _____

_____

_____

_____

✳ ✳ ✳ ✳

Website: _____

Username: _____

Password: _____

Notes: _____

_____

_____

_____

✳ ✳ ✳ ✳

Website: _____

Username: _____

Password: _____

Notes: _____

_____

_____

_____